Head for Home
Reading, Grade 1

Contents

Introduction 1
Stories and Exercises
My Friend Judy...2
Rosa's Letter Friend...................................4
Nan Mouse Rides.......................................6
A Nap for Pig...8
The Flying Turtle 10
Go to Sleep! 12
My Chick 14
Not in the Morning 16
Ham and Cheese 18
A Red Boat 20
Toot the Tugboat 22
Marco's Day...24
The Boat Ride 26

Far Away Places.......................................28
Just in Time..30
Baby Cakes 32
Best Friends 34
Cap Gets a Garden...................................36
What Frog Needed 38
Can You Find My Dog? 40
Fun Pages
Riddle Time! 42
Homophone Path......................................43
Hidden Picture 44
Knock, Knock!..45
Award Certificate...................................46
Answer Key...47

Introduction

Learning to read is clearly one of the most important things your child will ever do. By the first grade, most children are discovering the many skills they need to become confident readers. The skill that must go hand in hand with learning to read, however, is reading comprehension. When a child reads without understanding, he or she will quickly lose the joy that was discovered when each word began to make sense. Readers need to develop the skill of making sense of new words through context. They need to understand an author's message. They need to see how each event in a story affects the rest of the story and its characters. These are all important skills that must be practiced if a child is to become a successful reader.

This book will help your child achieve reading success. The short stories are a mix of fiction and nonfiction. The stories are fun, and the one-page exercises are varied. Without feeling the pressure of a long story to remember or many pages of exercises to work, your child will develop a better understanding of the content and have fun doing it!

Helping Your Child with Reading Comprehension
- Listen to your child read the stories several times. Ask questions to help your child understand the meaning of the story.
- Encourage your child to reread the stories frequently to gain additional confidence.
- Help your child find the meanings of difficult words through the context of the story. Practice the new words with your child. Use the words in other sentences.
- Go over the directions for the exercises together.
- Check the lesson when it is complete. Note areas of improvement as well as concern.

Thank you for being involved with your child's learning. A strong reading foundation will lead to a lifetime of reading enjoyment and success.

My Friend Judy
by Patricia Ann Becker

Hi! My name is Happy. I am a d[...]
a friend. Her name is Judy. She is a girl.

One day I took Judy out for a walk. We were having fun on our walk. I think she liked it when I ran away from her.

I was having so much fun running. Then I ran into the mud. Judy ran into the mud, too. She didn't like the mud very much.

"Don't run away from me any more!" she said.

Judy had mud all over her. I was glad that she took a bath. I was not glad when I had to get a bath. I just hate baths!

I think I will keep Judy. She is a good friend. She does just what I say. I do just what she says. We like each other.

Judy is my best friend. I think I am her best friend, too.

2

1. H_____ ____ ____ ____ ____ ____.

　　　dogs　　　friends　　　sisters

2. Judy ____ ____ ____ ____ ____ ____ ____ ____.

　　　girl　　　fun　　　bites

3. Judy and Happy run into the ____ ____ ____ ____ ____ ____.

　　　mud　　　house　　　shelf

4. Judy tells Happy not to ____ ____ ____ ____ ____ ____.

　　　run　　　hide　　　jump

5. Happy does not like ____ ____ ____ ____ ____ ____.

　　　running　　　walks　　　baths

6. Happy thinks he will ____ ____ ____ ____ ____ Judy.

　　　feed　　　keep　　　miss

Rosa's Letter Friend
by Jeanette Mara

Donna and Rosa wrote a [lot of letters] to each other. In one letter, [ ] asked Rosa to visit her when school [was out.]

Donna lived at the beach. [It was far] away. Rosa's mother needed t[o find] someone to care for the anim[als. She] needed to think about how she and Rosa could make the trip.

One morning Mother surprised Rosa. "I think we can go. I will ask our friends to feed our animals."

"Oh, I'm so happy!" said Rosa. "I'm going to meet my letter friend!"

The trip took a very long time. Mother said, "Next time, Donna can visit you. She can see your house."

When Rosa got to Donna's house, Donna was waiting. "Here is a rose for you, Rosa," Donna said. "I'm glad you could visit me."

"I'm glad, too," said Rosa. "I'm glad we are letter friends, and I'm glad we are friends."

1. When does Rosa visit Donna?
   Ⓐ when school starts
   Ⓑ when it is very cold
   Ⓒ when school is out

2. Where does Donna live?
   Ⓐ at the beach
   Ⓑ in the city
   Ⓒ at the farm

3. Who will Mother ask to feed the animals?
   Ⓐ Donna
   Ⓑ Rosa
   Ⓒ friends

4. How does Rosa feel when Mother tells her they can go on the trip?
   Ⓐ sad
   Ⓑ happy
   Ⓒ scared

5. What does Donna give Rosa?
   Ⓐ a rose
   Ⓑ an animal
   Ⓒ a letter

Nan Mouse Rides
by Jeanette Mara

"Do you like your birthday cake?"
Mother Mouse said.

"Yes," Nan Mouse said. "I like my cake very much!"

"Are you happy to have a birthday?"
Father Mouse said.

"Yes," Nan said. "I like growing up."

"This is for you," Father said, "and this is, too."

A backpack and a blue cap! Nan was so happy!

"We also have a pony ride for you," said Mother.

"Come see your pony!" said Father.

"I am so happy with this pony," Nan said. "I can ride this pony all day!"

Friends came to see the pony. They all wanted to ride the pony. So Nan let her friends have rides. Her friends were very happy. And Nan was very happy, too! Nan and her friends had fun with the pony all day.

1. Nan Mouse likes her birthday _____.

cake   song   money

2. Nan likes _____ up.

sitting   growing   showing

3. Mother and Father give Nan a blue cap and a
_____.

puppy   balloon   backpack

4. Mother and Father also give Nan a
_____.

car   pony   bird

5. Nan's friends come to _____
her pony.   see   read   hear

6. Nan's friends _____ the pony.

wash   ride   feed

A Nap for Pig
by Marie Richards

"Pig," said Mom, "come in for a nap."

"I don't like naps," said Pig. "I wish I could play all day!"

"You can't play all day," said Mom.

"I wish I were a bird. A bird could fly away and not nap," said Pig.

"You are not a bird," said Mom.

"I wish I were a frog. A frog could get wet and not nap," said Pig.

"You are not a frog," said Mom.

"I wish I were a fox. A fox could run away and not nap," said Pig.

"You are not a fox," said Mom. "I wish I were a horse."

"You do?" said Pig.

"Yes, I do!" said Mom. "A horse could TROT you to bed for a nap!"

"You can be a horse," said Pig. "You can trot me to bed."

"Jump on!" said Mom. "The horse will trot you to bed!"

Word List

jumps	nap	trots
wet	wishes	

1. Pig does not want to <u>sleep for a short time</u>.

---

2. Pig <u>wants very much</u> to be a fox.

---

3. Mom <u>runs slowly</u> with Pig to the bed.

---

4. Pig <u>moves through the air</u> onto Mom's back.

---

5. Pig wants to get <u>covered with water</u>.

The Flying Turtle
by Tanner Ottley Gay

One day Eagle said, "Turtle, I will take you flying."

Turtle climbed up on Eagle's back.

"Hold on," said Eagle. "Don't let go!" Up, up they flew.

"I'm flying! I'm flying!" Turtle yelled.

Many of Turtle's friends were down on the beach. "Look at Turtle!" they said.

When Turtle saw his friends, he just didn't think. He did not hold on the way he should have.

"Hello, down there!" he yelled.

"Turtle! Oh, no!" said Eagle.

Down went Turtle into the water. PLOP! Eagle flew down to the water quickly.

"Are you OK, Turtle?" she asked.

"Yes, Eagle," said Turtle. "But my flying days are over!"

After that day Turtle always says, "Take it from me. What you can do is better than something you can't do!"

1. Eagle takes Turtle _____.

swimming   flying   climbing

2. Eagle tells Turtle to _____.

hold on   let go   jump down

3. Turtle's friends watch him from the _____.

water   sky   beach

4. Turtle does not _____ and falls off.

fly   think   yell

5. Turtle falls into the _____.

water   ice   nest

6. Turtle says his flying _____ are over.

friends   days   back

Go to Sleep!
by Tanner Ottley Gay

All the birds were tired and wanted to go to sleep. But Little Bird wanted to play.

Grandma Bird went over to Little Bird. "You and I can play Keep Awake."

"Keep Awake? I've never played that," said Little Bird.

Grandma Bird said, "To play Keep Awake, we both have to be up all night. No sleeping at all!"

"This will be fun," said Little Bird. "How do you play?"

"You hum to yourself as I tweet to you. Then, when I stop tweeting, you tweet while I hum," she said.

Little Bird started humming, and Grandma Bird started tweeting. She tweeted and tweeted. He hummed and hummed.

Grandma Bird stopped tweeting. "Little Bird," she said, "now you can tweet and I'll hum."

But Little Bird was fast asleep.

1. What do Little Bird and Grandma Bird do?

Ⓐ go to sleep

Ⓑ play a game

Ⓒ read a story

2. Grandma Bird and Little Bird must _____.

Ⓐ eat dinner

Ⓑ fly away

Ⓒ stay awake all night

3. The players in the game must _____.

Ⓐ tweet and hum

Ⓑ sing and dance

Ⓒ jump and run

4. Who tweets first?

Ⓐ Little Bird

Ⓑ Grandma Bird

Ⓒ Little Bird and Grandma Bird

5. What does Little Bird do?

Ⓐ stays up all night

Ⓑ wins the game

Ⓒ falls asleep

My Chick
by Richard Christopher

Jill and Pam went swimming. "I can swim on this chick," said Jill.

"I can swim on a chick, too," said Pam.

Jill and Pam got out to play. "I am digging a hole with this shell," said Jill.

"I see a shell," said Pam. "I will get it."

Pam came back with no shell. "Where's the shell?" asked Jill.

"I pulled and pulled, but I couldn't get it," said Pam.

"Let ME try," said Jill.

They went back to the shell.

Jill pulled on it. "I can't get it," said Jill.

Pam said, "I will dig and you pull."

"Look, Pam!" said Jill. "Here are a lot of shells. What can we do?"

"We can make chicks," said Jill. "Here is my chick."

"Here is my chick, too!" said Pam.

14

Word List	dig	shell	pull
	swim	holes	

1. Pam tries to <u>grab and move</u> the shell.

_____

_ _ _ _ _ _ _ _ _ _ _ _ _ _ _ _ _

_____

2. The girls are making <u>openings</u> in the sand.

_____

_ _ _ _ _ _ _ _ _ _ _ _ _ _ _ _ _

_____

3. Pam and Jill <u>break up the sand</u> with a shell.

_____

_ _ _ _ _ _ _ _ _ _ _ _ _ _ _ _ _

_____

4. They <u>move in the water by using their arms and legs</u>.

_____

_ _ _ _ _ _ _ _ _ _ _ _ _ _ _ _ _

_____

5. The girls find a <u>hard outer covering</u>.

_____

_ _ _ _ _ _ _ _ _ _ _ _ _ _ _ _ _

_____

Not in the Morning
by Richard Christopher

Max and Dan went out to play. "What can we play this morning?" asked Dan.

"Let's play tag," said Max.

"You can play, but not me, not in the morning!" said Dan.

"Let's play Run Away, Fox," said Max.

"You can play, but not me, not in the morning!" said Dan.

"Let's play Green Men," said Max.

"You can play, but not me, not in the morning!" said Dan.

"Let's play Run Up, Run Down," said Max.

"You can play, but not me, not in the morning!" said Dan.

"Where did you go, Dan?" asked Max. "How can we play?"

"Here I am. Can you see me?" asked Dan.

"Not in the morning!" said Max.

16

1. Who is NOT playing outside?
Ⓐ Max
Ⓑ fox
Ⓒ Dan

2. What game does Max want to play first?
Ⓐ tag
Ⓑ Green Men
Ⓒ Run Up, Run Down

3. Dan says he does not want to play _____.
Ⓐ in the afternoon
Ⓑ in the morning
Ⓒ at night

4. How many games does Max name that he and Dan can play?
Ⓐ two
Ⓑ three
Ⓒ four

5. What game do you think Dan wants to play?
Ⓐ Run Away, Fox
Ⓑ hide-and-seek
Ⓒ tag

17

Ham and Cheese
by Carol Peske

"Let's go out for a day," said Cat.

"Yes, let's get out of the house," said Dog.

"What will we bring?" asked Cat.

"What can we dream up?" asked Dog.

"I'll bring cheese," said Cat.

"I don't like cheese," said Dog. "I'll bring ham."

"I don't like ham," said Cat.

"If you'll try the ham, I'll try the cheese," said Dog.

"If you'll try the cheese, I'll try the ham," said Cat.

"We can try the ham and cheese together," said Dog.

So Dog put cheese on the ham. And Cat put ham on the cheese.

"Mmm," said Dog.

"Mmm," said Cat.

"We like cheese AND ham," they said. "We will take both with us. We are all set. Let's go!"

18

Word List

cheese	dream up	together
try	house	

1. Cat and Dog want to get out of the <u>building where</u> _____

   <u>they live</u> for a while. _____

2. Dog says they can take whatever they can <u>picture in</u> _____

   <u>their minds</u>. _____

3. Cat will bring <u>a food made from milk</u>. _____

   _____

4. Cat and Dog will <u>test</u> the foods they don't like. _____

   _____

5. Dog and Cat will eat ham and cheese <u>with one</u> _____

   <u>another</u>. _____

19

A Red Boat
by Tanner Ottley Gay

Rick and Jill stopped to look at little boats in the water.

"Look at all the boats," said Rick sadly. "I want a boat, too!"

"If you would like a boat, we can make one," said Jill.

"But how?" asked Rick.

"I'll tell you when we get back to the house," said Jill. "Come on."

"This box will be our boat," said Jill after they were home.

"How can that be a boat?" said Rick.

"Like this," said Jill. "What kind of boat do you want?" asked Jill.

"I want a red boat," said Rick.

"Then we will make a red boat," said Jill. She cut the box open so they could make the boat.

Jill and Rick went back with their finished boat and put it in the water. A girl and her friends said, "What a good boat!"

"Thanks!" said Jill and Rick.

1. What kind of boats do Jill and Rick see in the water?

Ⓐ little

Ⓑ big

Ⓒ red

2. Why is Rick sad?

Ⓐ He wants to go home.

Ⓑ He wants a boat.

Ⓒ Jill is being mean to him.

3. What does Jill use to make a boat?

Ⓐ another boat

Ⓑ a house

Ⓒ a box

4. What color does Jill paint the boat?

Ⓐ red

Ⓑ blue

Ⓒ yellow

5. Where do Jill and Rick take their boat?

Ⓐ to their house

Ⓑ to a friend's home

Ⓒ to the water

Toot the Tugboat
by Carol Peske

Toot the Tugboat had been pulling big ships up the river for a long, long time. But now Toot was just too old. Toot was sad, but he also knew that he couldn't pull ships anymore. Many people came to see Toot one last time.

A man was out near the docks. Seeing the line of people made him think of a way to save Toot. "Look how many people are lining up to see Toot one last time. Don't you think people would line up to see him every day?" asked the man.

"Yes," said a woman. "I think people would come to see a real tugboat."

"I like it!" said the man who ran Toot. "Toot could stay here, and people could come to see him."

"Toot the Tugboat is saved! We love you, Toot the Tugboat!" yelled the people.

"Toot the Tugboat loves you, too," said Toot.

1. Toot the Tugboat had pulled _____.

docks   ships   rivers

2. Many _____ lined up to see Toot.

people   tugboats   cars

3. A man near the docks thought of a way to

_____ Toot.

pull   save   run

4. The man who ran Toot was happy that Toot could

_____ there.

stay   play   see

5. The people _____ Toot the Tugboat.

found   missed   loved

6. Toot had many _____.

rivers   friends   times

23

Marco's Day
by Patricia Ann Becker

While we were eating dinner, I began telling Mom and Dad about my day. "The paper said good morning to me," I began. "At school, I saw a bug with a hat on."

"Oh," said my mom.

"That's nice," said my dad.

"Then I saw a shell tree on my way home," I said.

Mom and Dad just smiled.

Just then the paper began to talk. "Hello, Marco! How are you?" it said.

"I'm fine," I said, smiling.

Then a bug with a hat on climbed up Dad's sleeve. "That bug has a hat on!" yelled Dad.

"Yes, I know," I said.

Next, a shell tree walked in and gave us each a shell.

"Now I believe you," said my mom.

"Me, too!" said my dad.

"At last!" I laughed. "What a silly day this has been!"

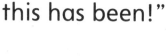

24

Word List

yell	dinner	climbs
laughs	sleeve	

1. The bug was on the <u>cloth that covers part of the arm</u>.

   ----

2. Marco <u>makes sounds that show happiness</u> when he tells his mom and dad about his day.

   ----

3. Dad does <u>cry out</u> when he sees the bug.

   ----

4. The family is eating its <u>main meal of the day</u>.

   ----

5. The bug <u>moves up using its legs</u> on Dad.

The Boat Ride
by Liane B. Onish

Fran and Dot are friends. They looked down from the top tree branch.

"I see boats," said Fran. "I see a blue boat, and I see a green boat. We can go for boat rides."

"Let's go, Fran!" said Dot.

They jumped down from the branch.

"The boats are big," said Fran. "I can't lift the blue boat."

"I can't lift the green boat," said Dot.

"Can we both lift the blue boat?" said Fran.

"Yes, we can!" said Dot.

"Now we will both lift the green boat," said Fran.

"We did it!" said Dot.

"You have the green boat. Get in!" said Fran.

"You have the blue boat. Get in!" said Dot.

Fran and Dot climbed into the boats. Then the happy friends went for a ride.

1. How many boats does Fran see?
Ⓐ one
Ⓑ two
Ⓒ three

2. Where do Fran and Dot jump?
Ⓐ from the boats
Ⓑ from the branch
Ⓒ from the water

3. Which boat did Fran and Dot lift first?
Ⓐ the blue boat
Ⓑ the green boat
Ⓒ the red boat

4. Which boat did Fran have?
Ⓐ the yellow boat
Ⓑ the green boat
Ⓒ the blue boat

5. Where did the friends go?
Ⓐ for a boat ride
Ⓑ for a swim
Ⓒ for a plane ride

Far Away Places
by Beverley Dietz

Let's have some fun. Close your eyes. Think about a place you want to visit. Let's go!

Maybe you want to visit a place that is cold. You could play in the snow and have fun on the ice. You might want to go for a long ride.

Maybe you want to go to a place that is hot. You might find sand. But you might not find water.

Some big animals live in some hot lands. Would you like to ride on one of them?

Some places get a lot of rain. Do you wish to go to a place like that? You could see very big trees and many animals.

Maybe you want to go very, very far away. You might want to visit space and see a star close. Maybe someday you will!

28

Word List

sand	stars	fun
rain	visit	

1. You can have <u>enjoyment</u> thinking about places to go.

_____

- - - - - - - - - - - - - - - - -

_____

2. Think of places you want to <u>go to see</u>.

_____

- - - - - - - - - - - - - - - - -

_____

3. You may walk on <u>tiny crushed rocks</u> in some hot places.

_____

- - - - - - - - - - - - - - - - -

_____

4. Trees need <u>water that falls in drops from the clouds</u>.

_____

- - - - - - - - - - - - - - - - -

_____

5. There are many <u>bodies in the sky that shine</u> in space.

_____

- - - - - - - - - - - - - - - - -

_____

Just in Time
by Nancy Ray

House Mouse came out of his house. He saw Garden Mouse in the garden.

"Come and play!" said Garden Mouse.

House Mouse said, "It's fun in the garden. It's fun to have a friend, too."

"Look at all that we can eat," said Garden Mouse.

House Mouse was about to eat. But he stopped just in time. House Mouse saw a cat.

"A cat is here!" he said. "Come with me!"

House Mouse and Garden Mouse ran back to the house. The cat ran to the house.

House Mouse jumped through a window and down. Garden Mouse jumped down. The cat jumped down, too.

House Mouse and Garden Mouse ran into the mouse hole, just in time!

"I'm happy to have a friend and have fun," said House Mouse. "But next time, we could have all the fun in here."

1. House Mouse and Garden Mouse are

_____

- -

_____.

    cats   friends   enemies

2. House Mouse and Garden Mouse

_____

- -

_____ in the garden.

    play   sleep   plant

3. House Mouse _____ a cat.

          eats   sees   jumps

4. House Mouse and Garden Mouse run into the mouse

_____

- -

_____.

    garden   fence   hole

5. The cat _____ through a window.

    jumps   walks   stops

6. Next time, House Mouse wants to play in the

_____

- -

_____.

    garden   house   window

Baby Cakes
by Liane B. Onish

"Why are you sad?" Mother says.

"Alex can't come out to play," I tell her. "His mother wants him to play with the baby. Now what can I do?" I say to Mother.

"What can you and I do that is fun?" she says. Mother sits down and thinks with me.

"I think I know what you and I can do," Mother says. "We know how to make a cake. Let's make little cakes for Alex and the baby."

"Yes, let's do that!" I say. "Let's make baby cakes. Alex and the baby will like them."

Mother and I go to see Alex. We have little cakes for my best friend and for the baby.

Alex and the baby like the little cakes. Now everybody is happy!

1. Why is the boy sad?

Ⓐ His friend is sick.

Ⓑ His friend is making cakes.

Ⓒ His friend cannot play.

2. What does Alex's mother want him to do?

Ⓐ play with the baby

Ⓑ clean his room

Ⓒ make a cake

3. Who has the idea to make cakes?

Ⓐ the baby

Ⓑ Mother

Ⓒ Alex

4. Where do the boy and his mother go?

Ⓐ to see a movie

Ⓑ to see Alex

Ⓒ to the store

5. How does the boy feel at the end of story?

Ⓐ sick

Ⓑ sad

Ⓒ happy

Best Friends
by Tanner Ottley Gay

One day, Rick sat at the table. "Why are you sad?" asked Chen.

"My mom and dad said we are going to get a big house," said Rick.

"Why did they say that?" asked Chen. "Don't they like your house?"

"Our house is not big," said Rick. "With the baby, we will not all fit in our house."

"Where will you go?" asked Chen.

"We will go to a house that is bigger than our house is," said Rick.

The best friends got up. "I will not see you," said Chen. "I'm sad."

Rick said, "I'm sad, too. But you can come and play for a day. We can make new friends. And MY friends are YOUR friends. Then we will have lots of friends!"

"Now I'm not sad," said Chen. "I'm glad. We are best friends, Rick!"

"You bet we are!" said Rick.

34

Directions Read each sentence. Choose a word from the
Word List that has the same meaning as the
underlined words. Write the word on the line.

Word List

glad   table   too

baby   big

1. The two boys are sitting at a <u>piece of furniture that
has a flat top with legs under it</u>.

_____

- - - - - - - - - - - - - - - - - -

_____

2. Rick's family has a <u>very young child</u>.

_____

- - - - - - - - - - - - - - - - - -

_____

3. Rick is moving to a house that is <u>great in size</u>.

_____

- - - - - - - - - - - - - - - - - -

_____

4. When Rick is sad, Chen is sad <u>also</u>.

_____

- - - - - - - - - - - - - - - - - -

_____

5. Rick and Chen are <u>happy</u> that they are best friends.

_____

- - - - - - - - - - - - - - - - - -

_____

Cap Gets a Garden
by Beverley Dietz

"Cap and I went for a walk," Pat said. "We saw some gardens. I think Cap likes gardens. Could we have a garden?"

"Cap likes gardens?" asked Dad. "Cap is a dog. What makes you think Cap wants a garden?"

"Let's go out," Pat said. "You will see. Cap likes gardens." Cap looked happy.

Dad and Pat went out of the house. Cap went, too. "We could plant a garden here," Pat said. "Cap can help."

Dad just looked at Pat. Then Cap began to dig. "Now I see!" said Dad. "Cap does want a garden!" Then Dad and Pat began to help Cap dig.

The next day, what do you think they did? They planted a garden of their own.

"Do you like this garden?" Pat asked Cap. She thinks he does!

1. Who went for a walk?

Ⓐ Cap and Dad

Ⓑ Cap and Pat

Ⓒ Pat and Dad

2. What did Pat and Cap see?

Ⓐ dogs

Ⓑ gardens

Ⓒ stores

3. What does Pat want to do?

Ⓐ take Dad for a walk

Ⓑ cut some flowers

Ⓒ plant a garden

4. How does Cap show that he wants a garden?

Ⓐ He begins to dig.

Ⓑ He barks at Dad.

Ⓒ He lies down.

5. Where do Pat, Dad, and Cap plant their garden?

Ⓐ at the park

Ⓑ inside the house

Ⓒ outside the house

What Frog Needed
by Torré Montero

A frog woke up one morning. He looked up and then down. Worms and a fly were in the frog's dish. In the frog's box were water and some rocks to sit on, too. The frog could see other animals in the pet shop.

The frog saw a man at the front of the pet shop who came to work every morning. He began to look after the animals.

The man opened the box the frog lived in to put in more food. Just then a mother and a boy came into the pet shop. They wanted to look at one of the mice.

The man stopped what he was doing and got out the mouse. The mouse was the one the boy said he needed.

That's when the frog saw what it needed and it wasn't food and it wasn't water. This frog wanted to go outdoors.

The frog hopped out of the box and into the outdoors. That was what the frog needed!

Directions Choose the word that best fits each sentence. Write the word on the line.

1. The main character of the story is a

_____

- - - - - - - - - - - - - - - - - - - -

_____.

       worm   fly   frog

2. The frog lives in a _____.

              house   box   rock

3. A _____ takes care of the animals.

   man   mother   boy

4. A mother and a boy want to see a

_____

- - - - - - - - - - - - - - - - - - - -

_____.

      frog   mouse   box

5. The frog _____ outdoors.

      runs   flies   hops

6. The story takes place in the

_____

- - - - - - - - - - - - - - - - - - - -

_____.

    morning   outdoors   water

Can You Find My Dog?
by Liane B. Onish

The sun came up. Big Dog climbed up on the bed. Big Dog went off the bed and out the window.

Cam went to find Big Dog. "I do not see my dog," said Cam.

Was Big Dog in the doghouse? Cam went to the doghouse. Big Dog was not in the doghouse. "I cannot find my dog," said Cam.

Was Big Dog in the barn? Cam went to the barn. Big Dog was not in the barn. "I cannot find my dog," said Cam.

Was Big Dog on the big hill? Cam climbed up. Big Dog was not on top. "I cannot find my dog," said Cam.

Cam did not see Big Dog. "I cannot find my dog," said Cam.

Cam went back. Big Dog was on the bed. "I did find my dog," said Cam.

Word List

top	barn	sun
bed	window	

1. The <u>star that gives light and heat</u> comes up in the

_____

- - - - - - - - - - - - - - - - - -

morning. _____

2. Big Dog went out the <u>opening in a wall</u>.

_____

- - - - - - - - - - - - - - - - - -

_____

3. Cam looked for Big Dog in the <u>building that is used</u>

_____

- - - - - - - - - - - - - - - - - -

<u>to keep cows and horses</u>. _____

4. Big Dog was not on the <u>highest part</u> of the hill.

_____

- - - - - - - - - - - - - - - - - -

_____

5. Cam found Big Dog on her <u>place where she sleeps</u>.

_____

- - - - - - - - - - - - - - - - - -

_____

Riddle Time!

Directions ➤ **Share these riddles with your friends and family.**

1. What do you get when you chop down a tuna tree?
   (fish sticks)

2. What did one tornado say to the other tornado?
   (Let's blow this town.)

3. What do sharks eat with peanut butter?
   (jellyfish)

4. Where does a ghost look up words?
   (in a diction-eerie)

5. Why did Spiderman get a computer?
   (so he could find the World Wide Web)

6. What do fish like to paint with?
   (watercolors)

7. Who can hold up a school bus with one hand?
   (a crossing guard)

8. How many letters are in the alphabet?
   (11 letters are in <u>the alphabet</u>)

Homophone Path

Homophones are words that sound the same but have different spellings. **To** and **two** are homophones.

Directions Find a homophone partner for each word in the Word List. Draw a line to connect the homophone partners and help Kitty follow the path to her friends.

Word List   blue   here   eight   meet

write

sea

too

blew

ate

hear

meat

fun

Hidden Picture

Directions Color each part that names an animal.
A picture will appear!

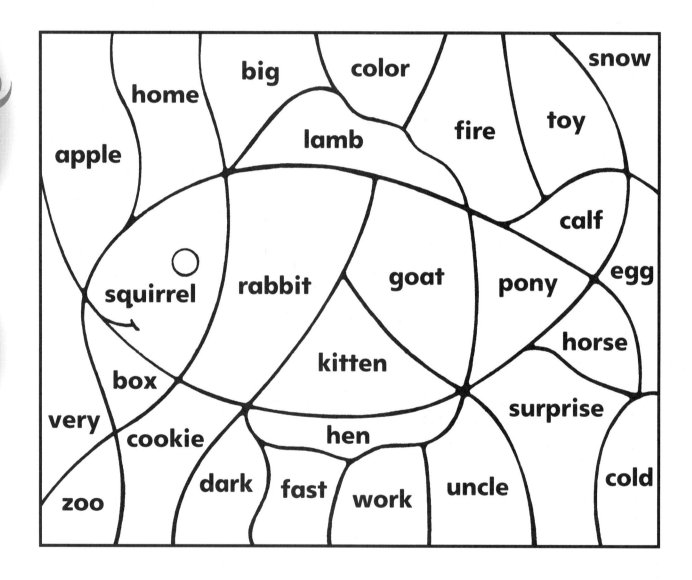

Knock, Knock!

Directions ▸ Break the secret code by using the key below. Write a letter above each number.

A	B	C	D	E	F	G	H	I	J	K	L	M	N	O	P	Q	R	S	T	U	V	W	X	Y	Z
1	2	3	4	5	6	7	8	9	10	11	12	13	14	15	16	17	18	19	20	21	22	23	24	25	26

KNOCK, KNOCK!

___ ___ ___   ___ ___   ___ ___ ___ ___ ___?
23   8   15   9   19   20   8   5   18   5

___ ___ ___ ___ ___ ___.
2   1   14   1   14   1

___ ___ ___ ___ ___ ___   ___ ___ ___?
2   1   14   1   14   1   23   8   15

KNOCK, KNOCK!

___ ___ ___   ___ ___   ___ ___ ___ ___ ___?
23   8   15   9   19   20   8   5   18   5

___ ___ ___ ___ ___ ___.
2   1   14   1   14   1

___ ___ ___ ___ ___ ___   ___ ___ ___?
2   1   14   1   14   1   23   8   15

KNOCK, KNOCK!

___ ___ ___   ___ ___   ___ ___ ___ ___ ___?
23   8   15   9   19   20   8   5   18   5

___ ___ ___ ___ ___ ___.
15   18   1   14   7   5

___ ___ ___ ___ ___ ___   ___ ___ ___?
15   18   1   14   7   5   23   8   15

___ ___ ___ ___ ___ ___   ___ ___ ___
15   18   1   14   7   5   25   15   21

___ ___ ___ ___   ___   ___ ___ ___
7   12   1   4   9   4   9   4

___ ___ ___   ___ ___ ___
14   15   20   19   1   25

___ ___ ___ ___ ___ ___?
2   1   14   1   14   1

2036

45

© Steck-Vaughn

Congratulations!

This award certifies that

_____

is a Super Reader!

Super Reader

Head for Home
Reading, Grade 1
Answer Key

Page 3
1. friends
2. fun
3. mud
4. run
5. baths
6. keep

Page 5
1. C
2. A
3. C
4. B
5. A

Page 7
1. cake
2. growing
3. backpack
4. pony
5. see
6. ride

Page 9
1. nap
2. wishes
3. trots
4. jumps
5. wet

Page 11
1. flying
2. hold on
3. beach
4. think
5. water
6. days

Page 13
1. B
2. C
3. A
4. B
5. C

Page 15
1. pull
2. holes
3. dig
4. swim
5. shell

Page 17
1. B
2. A
3. B
4. C
5. B

Page 19
1. house
2. dream up
3. cheese
4. try
5. together

Page 21
1. A
2. B
3. C
4. A
5. C

Page 23
1. ships
2. people
3. save
4. stay
5. loved
6. friends

Page 25
1. sleeve
2. laughs
3. yell
4. dinner
5. climbs

Page 27
1. B
2. B
3. A
4. C
5. A

Page 29
1. fun
2. visit
3. sand
4. rain
5. stars

Page 31
1. friends
2. play
3. sees
4. hole
5. jumps
6. house

Page 33
1. C
2. A
3. B
4. B
5. C

Page 35
1. table
2. baby
3. big
4. too
5. glad

Page 37
1. B
2. B
3. C
4. A
5. C

Page 39
1. frog
2. box
3. man
4. mouse
5. hops
6. morning

Page 41
1. sun
2. window
3. barn
4. top
5. bed

Page 43
Connect blew, hear, ate, and meat.

Page 44
Color lamb, squirrel, rabbit, goat, kitten, pony, calf, horse, and hen.

Page 45
KNOCK, KNOCK!
WHO IS THERE?
BANANA.
BANANA WHO?
KNOCK, KNOCK!
WHO IS THERE?
BANANA.
BANANA WHO?
KNOCK, KNOCK!
WHO IS THERE?
ORANGE.
ORANGE WHO?
ORANGE YOU GLAD I
DID NOT SAY BANANA?